HOUSES OF PUEBLA

THE CRADLE OF MEXICAN ARCHITECTURE

Angelopolitana Ciuitas

HOUSES OF PUEBLA

THE CRADLE OF MEXICAN ARCHITECTURE

Marie-Pierre Colle

Photography
Ignacio Urquiza

Translation from the Spanish
Maki Winkelmann

The Vendome Press
New York   Paris

Published in the USA in 1998 by
The Vendome Press
1370 Avenue of the Americas
New York, NY 10019

Distributed in the USA and Canada by
Rizzoli International Publications
through St. Martin's Press
175 Fifth Avenue
New York, NY 10010

Author:	Marie-Pierre Colle
Photographer:	Ignacio Urquiza
Design:	Martín Jon García-Urtiaga
	Lucila Flores de Clavé
Research and Texts:	Marie-Pierre Colle
	Erendira de la Lama
	Francisco Miranda
Production Assistants:	Carla Zarebska
	Stacey Symonds
Copy Editor:	Bertha Ruiz de la Concha
Translation:	Maki Winkelmann
Assistant Photographer:	René López

Library of Congress Cataloging-in-Publication Data

Colle, Marie-Pierre
    Puebla: the cradle of Mexican architecture / Marie-Pierre Colle.
       p. cm.
    Includes bibliographical references.
    ISBN 0-86565-966-4 (hc)
      1. Architecture--Mexico--Puebla--Themes, motives. 2. Puebla
(Mexico)--Social life and customs. I. Title.
    NA757. P8C65 1998
    720' . 972' 48--dc21   97-28293
    Printed in Singapore by Toppan Printing Company   CIP

Table of Contents

To Puebla
To my son Eric
To the Thursday Writers' Workshop

Acknowledgments

I would first like to thank my friends, Maye de Milmo, Jorge García Murillo of the Museo de Monterrey and Ricardo Guajardo Touché from Bancomer who unconditionally supported and sponsored the first edition of *Casa Poblana*. The Government of the State of Puebla helped with the research. Dr. Sabino Yano first had the idea for this book. The long walks through the streets of Puebla —day and night— discovering patios, nooks and neighborhoods, were catalysts that got the project off the ground. Without him, much of the flavor of Puebla might not have been grasped.

Mario de la Torre, so generous with his time, guided and gave advice to *Casa Poblana* from the beginning.

I thank Claudio and Ana Luisa Landucci, Miguel and Sonia Mancera, Mónica del Villar, Martha Levy, Héctor Azar, Lupe Pérez Rivero y Maurer for their support, and the Thursday Writers' Workshop, particularly Alicia Trueba. Guillermo Tovar y de Teresa read the first draft of the introduction in Berlin.

Guillermo Grimm brought inspiration and enthusiasm to the development and creation of the book.

Professor Gonzalo Fernández Márquez introduced me to the *Casa de los Muñecos*. Architects Sergio Vergara and Ignacio Ibarra opened doors and windows to the architecture of Puebla as did Architect Mary Vázquez.

We spent several afternoons in the home of José Ignacio Conde while he told us stories about the old Puebla families and about the 18th and 19th centuries.

Dr. José Luis Pérez de Salazar lent us meaningful material for the research. He showed us how he fights to safeguard his own space in his Puebla style home in Mexico City, which overflows with cherished *objets*.

Doña Carmen Pérez de Salazar de Ovando allowed us to photograph a family portrait, as well as two of the finest inlaid desks, which my father —an art-dealer— particularly admired and loved to touch.

Pablo and Lisette Maurer's hospitality in the Atlixco wheat mill is unforgettable; I will always remember the aroma of a cup of coffee in San Mateo.

Thanks to María Eugenia Alvarez Murphy and Gabriel Alarcón for giving us access to the Hostal de Velasco, to the Amparo Foundation for allowing us to photograph its museum, to Alicia Araujo of the Bello Museum, to Professor Roberto Reyes of the Palafox Library and to the Bello Zetina Museum.

María Elena Landa introduced me into the Popolocan house and to the spectacular organ cacti forest near Tehuacán. She made me feel the Puebla style.

Javier Jiménez Brito brought his energy to *Casa Poblana*. Thanks to him, we took the pictures of the Reforma 517 house, with its splendid examples of *Art Nouveau* , *Art Deco,* neo-Gothic, neo-classical and romantic.

Juan Rangel Muñoz and his sister María Eugenia Rangel Muñoz allowed us to savor their 17th-century house, with its spectacular *Art Deco* patio, one of my favorites. José Esteban and Lidia Chapital showed us that the haciendas of yesterday can be the ideal setting for today's art and cabinetry.

Don José Cué treated us to the finest Puebla hospitality, as did Architect José Antonio Romano and Laura Caso Menéndez. Doña María Luisa Velasco de Matienzo lent us props for some photographs.

Architect Manolo Mestre was an ardent advisor of *Casa Poblana*. We toured Cuautinchán, Huejotzingo, Tecali and Tepeaca. Bettina Verut initiated us into the San Francisco festivities in Cuetzalan. Carlos Obregón and Cecilia Margaona introduced us to the *códice* and the Cuautinchán convent during the Feast of the Dead.

I thank Eric Giebeler, Roberta Lajous, Cristina Gálvez, Yvonne Tron, Enrique Torres Septién, René López, Juana Cruz, Rosalba Ramírez, Olivia Aruesti, Aurora García, Nidia Esquivel de Galán, Michael Calderwood, Maki Winkelmann and John Wiseman.

Martín Jon García-Urtiaga brought his talent and experience to the design. Lucila Flores is present on each page, as is Bertha Ruiz de la Concha.

I thank all those who allowed us to photograph their homes which, for lack of space, could not be included in the book.

Carla Zarebska and Stacey Symonds, faithful and eager assistants, brought vitality to the elaboration of *Casa Poblana*.

Eréndira de la Lama and Francisco Miranda researched the subject thoroughly, participating in the creation of *Casa Poblana* from the outset and maintaining their good humor, patience and enthusiasm throughout the project.

I thank CNCA-INAH for the use of the facilities in their Regional Center in Puebla and the National Archives.

Last but not least, I render homage to Ignacio Urquiza, to his sensitivity and to his excellent photographs. As we combed and explored the state of Puebla together, we forged a friendship which led us to create several more books.

I wish to express my enormous pleasure in having worked with this splendid team.

Marie-Pierre Colle
Tepotzlán, January 1993

11

Introduction

They say that a large cross appeared in the skies marking the site for Puebla. Angels then sketched a layout for the city. "Fabulous spectacle! Angels planting here as they measured there, achieving a heavenly harmony, befitting glory, unlike worldly art."

The story of Puebla is full of angels. During its construction, Queen Isabel of Portugal saw winged beings in her dreams, marking the site with string. In 1603, when a major flood devastated the city, they say that angels cleared away the mud during the night, so that people would not abandon the city. Years later, thanks to a miracle by Saint Michael the Archangel, water sprang forth from the mountains, ending a heavy drought. Another story relates that the bell María, twice broken in its journey to the cathedral tower, was healed by angels. "Weep bronze bell, weep bell María, in your resonance can be heard the voice of Motolinía."

Legend also holds that angels had a hand in building the Puebla cathedral. Each night, they raised its height by an amount equal to what had been built during the day. That is why the city bears the splendid name *Puebla de los Angeles* ... Puebla of the Angels.

History recounts that friars founded Puebla on April 16, 1530. The site —on the Veracruz-Mexico City route— had great potential for the socio-political project they conceived: a wholly Spanish city to contrast with nearby indigenous Tlaxcala. The area was ruled by a council of residents and was granted a special franchise from the Spanish Crown: a thirty year tax exemption and a hundred year exemption on excise and import-export duties.

Puebla was laid out as a grid with all the streets leading toward the four cardinal points, a model of Spanish Renaissance. Indigenous neighborhoods —which provided the labor force— were left on the outskirts.

Map of the city of Puebla by José Mariano de Medina, 1754. (National Archives)

Right: Rhythm of the arcade's Tuscan-style columns in the corridor of the Convento de la Concepción.

15

The Franciscans were the first of the monks to arrive; they were soon followed by the Augustinians and the Dominicans. By 1606 there were thirty convents, which were used as charitable institutions, retreat centers and hospitals, churches and schools. Because the City of Puebla had a mild climate, was safe and well-located, it became the capital of the province of Puebla — the largest of New Spain— extending from the Gulf of Mexico to the Pacific Ocean. It was also the Bishopric of Tlaxcala, which included Veracruz and extended south to Tabasco.

Puebla very quickly became the second largest city of the kingdom and its most important manufacturing center. Don Juan de Palafox y Mendoza is largely responsible for the city's greatness. He arrived early in the 17th century to do an audit for the Viceroy, then became the bishop of Puebla, the bishop of Mexico, Senior Inquisitor, Viceroy of New Spain, and Captain General of Guatemala. He strengthened the secular clergy, constructed the cathedral, founded seminaries, and built the famous library that bears his name.

Detail of a 16th-century Toltec-Chichimec manuscript —in the Nahuatl language— found in Cuautinchán. Both bed and chair are made of straw.

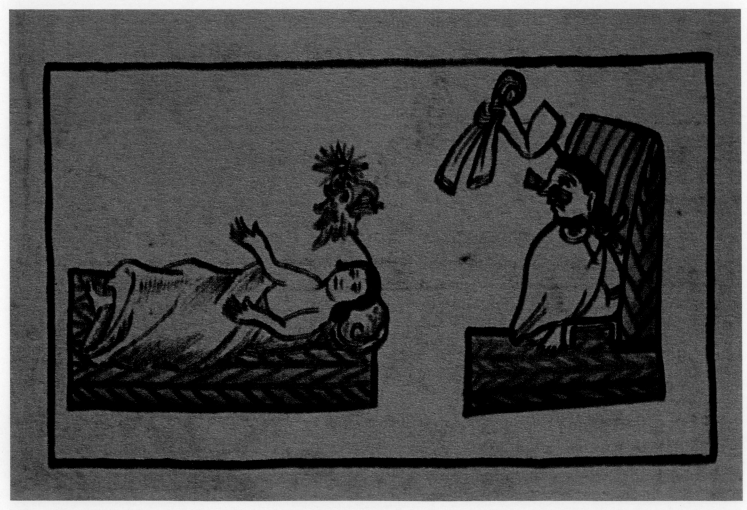

While Puebla has Spanish traditions and customs, the indigenous culture is alive in provincial towns such as Huejotzingo, Tepeaca and Cuetzalan, particularly during its festivals. Nearby Cholula had been a sacred city to many indigenous cultures. When the Spanish arrived, Cholula was inhabited by the Toltecs, although its pyramid was no longer a cult site. Spanish monks filled Cholula with domes and crosses. Finally, in the 18th century, they erected the *Templo de la Virgen de los Remedios* on the summit of the pyramid.

The visitor will quickly discover Puebla's hospitality: a plate of beans, from the cook's own harvest, made in a clay pot and served with freshly-made *tortillas* and little *tamales* wrapped in dried corn leaves and stuffed with *mole*, or chilies, or prepared as sweets. The Pre-Hispanic soul is still alive. At the center of the home is the hearth, its ever-glowing coals symbolizing the continuity of the life cycle.

The tallest pyramid in Mesoamerica lies in Cholula; Nuestra Señora de los Remedios church stands on its summit.

Local climate and materials dictate the architecture. In the Tehuacan area, the Popoloca house has *bajareque* walls and stone skirting. The thatch roof juts out beyond the tie beam to form a triangular opening, which serves as a smoke hatch and allows for ventilation. The grain is stored outside in a *cuescomate*, a giant pot-shaped adobe hut. In the Molcaxac area, houses are made of white stone.

In the mountains near Cuetzalan and Zacapoaxtla, the roofs are made of *tejamaníl*. Porch walls hung with potted plants are turned into gardens. Cuetzalan's colorful houses have a central patio encircled by a porch and a wooden second floor, roofed in tile, and trimmed with balconies.

A 17th-century visitor to the Izúcar area noted that "... the land is scorched by the sun and native homes are built of cane spikes with air flowing through at will, so that they seem more like cages than like houses."

A hybrid building style emerged as the native population borrowed ideas from the Spanish. They blended cut stone, adobe combined with stucco, beams, porches, windows and wooden doors, with their traditional techniques.

Peaceful country life: this indigenous house of the central zone blends into the landscape.

Right: Holy Week crosses on the road from Tetela to Ocampo.

*Hacienda*s were factories with vast expanses of land that produced the raw materials —wheat, sugar, agave or livestock— needed for their outputs. Their homes and installations were massive. Established in the 16th century, *hacienda*s were expanded over the next two hundred years; their productivity reached its zenith during the 18th century. By the 19th century, *hacienda*s had acquired the character of industrial plants.

The great sugar plantations at La Galarza, Colón, and San Nicolás Tolentino near Izúcar de Matamoros, had the capacity to process and transport their harvest.

The *haciendas* of the Puebla valley, irrigated by the runoff from volcanic glaciers, supplied grain to the whole of New Spain. The Atlixco area produced most of the wheat, spawning the greatest number of flour mills, like San Mateo.

The El Rijo sugar mill reached its pinnacle in the 19th century.

Hacienda architecture was simple at the start: barns, bays and enclosures built around a patio. As the landlords —the *hacendados*— became richer, they added comfort and luxury to their homes. Abandoning the fortress-style early on, they added arcades and corridors, balconies and cornices, as well as stone fountains. Oratories became chapels and in some cases, real churches.

The 19th-century economic boom ushered in by the railroads brought with it travel and trade and many new ideas. Puebla imitated and adopted the neoclassical, romantic, Mudéjar, and neo-Gothic styles, as its *hacienda*s were transformed into mansions that yearned to be English, French or ... Miramar. Puebla's eclectic style emerged.

Indigo blue adds character to the arch of a barn near Atlixco.

Next Pages: Headdresses worn by the Quetzal dancers at the San Francisco festival in Cuetzalan.

Puebla, pathway of dreams, is an essential stop for those who want a dose of authentic Mexico. Pueblans are proud of their history and protect their traditions and customs. Theirs is a heritage of inns at the crossroads; hospitality is one of their earliest habits. The large portals and heavy iron gates of Puebla can be opened easily.

Convents have played an important role in the life of Puebla since the 16th century. Apart from providing a home to the myriad priests and nuns who came to evangelize and colonize the area, they housed hospitals and inns, and many schools, where religion, manual skills and art were taught. The convents needed to have large kitchens.

Two convent kitchens stand out in the history of Puebla: the Santa Mónica —where the quintessential baroque dish, *chiles en nogada*, was created— and the Santa Rosa, where *mole* was invented in the year 1700.

History recounts that Bishop Manuel Fernández de Santa Cruz, awaiting a visit from the Viceroy, requested a special dish that would combine Mexican and Spanish cuisine. Sister Andrea de la Asunción, in charge of the Santa Rosa kitchen, chose the chile and the almond to represent the basic Mexican and Spanish ingredients. She then added sweet ingredients —plantain, chocolate and raisins— to subdue the fierce chile. She used sesame seeds and peanuts as thickeners, added cumin, cloves and cinnamon to round off the flavor, and included the elementals of Mexican cuisine, the onion, garlic and tomato. Tasting her creation, Sister Andrea pronounced the *mole* too heavy, and so she added anise and burned tortilla to aid digestion. In the end, the *mole* had sixteen ingredients and became a national dish.

Puebla's luscious delights can be traced to Moorish sweets. Every child loves the *conchas, chilindrinas, cocoles, jamoncillos, trompadas, muéganos, natillas, alfeñiques, canelones, mosquitos, alfajores, camotes* which fill confectionery shops decorated with cut paper designs and images of the Sacred Heart framed in tulle.

"Puebla, home of *camotes* and marzipan, made by the hands of Catarina of San Juan."

Every kitchen is alive with traditional utensils : *atole* jugs and pots to cook the beans, boil the milk, heat the water, make the rice and serve the *mole* as well as green glass jugs for *aguas frescas*, the fresh fruit drinks. The cornmeal *masa* awaits next to mortars,

The San Agustín ex-hacienda at the foot of the Popocatépetl volcano. The Iztaccíhuatl, the La Malinche and the Citlaltépetl are the other volcanoes encircling the Puebla valley.

25

big glass water bottles and chocolate grinders on counters trimmed in *azulejo* tiles. Arrieta captured the flavors in his paintings.

There is a parallel between Puebla architecture and its cuisine. The multitude of ingredients, the layering of elements, colors, textures and flavors, the *Casa de Alfeñique*, nougat, the wedding cake, embossed stucco, lintels and piers, turned pillars, the red and yellow of the walls, and the sauces with cream.

Puebla is a city of strong contrasts and severe colonial character, Spanish with an unmistakable Mudéjar imprint. Viewed from the Loreto fort, the city is a kaleidoscopic mosaic of flat roofs and orange domes flecked with terra-cotta and *talavera*. The sun in a land of mountains, a prayer to heaven, the silent song of stone and history.

Andalusian baroque statuary found a fertile land in Puebla. The fanciful combination of cupids, shells, flowered crests, turned pillars and winged spirits produced grandiose altar-pieces and façades. In Santa María Tonantzintla, in San Francisco Acatepec

A talavera tile sun shines on the tower of San Francisco Acatepec church.

Right: Santa María de Tonanzintla; a striking example of Churrigueresque art in New Spain.

26

and in the famous Chapel of the Rosary, the style became *Churrigueresque.* This influence is also present in the furniture inlaid with geometric patterns —stars and broken angles— in contrasting tropical woods, bone and ivory.

Puebla is a garden. Andalusian culture was planted and shaped by the personality of the land and the native labor. Time infused eastern and European ideas, but the result is a Mexican blossom, typically Puebla.

Puebla wanted to create a style to rival that of Mexico City. Façades were covered in clay and ceramics. The grid layout gave birth to *petatillo* and chess.

Puebla *azulejo* tile began when Castilian potters from Talavera de la Reina opened ceramics factories. The Far East had brought them the geometric patterns and stylized flower designs, traditionally blue-on-white. The *talavera* potters added yellow, green and oxide red. The result is a warm and understated symmetry, never strident.

Architecture reflects man's spiritual state. The city is the workshop of its inhabitants, its façades rows of book spines on a library shelf. Each house is a story, a genealogy, a moment. Some are trimmed with Xonaca stone, others with Cholula brick, or limestone from the Alera range, or sand from the Atoyac river. The great mansions embellish their arcades, lintels and piers, parapets and emblems. Leftover brick, stone and adobe are combined on "beggar" walls.

In the 16th century, two-storey houses were built on lands adjacent to the *Zócalo,* which were given to the conquistadors immediately after the founding of the city. They started as simple structures adopting the Mudéjar patio layout, window grilles and carved stone edging. The best examples of the era are the *Casa del Deán* and the *Casa del que Mató al Animal,* with a magnificent bas-relief in the arcade.

The 17th century brought greater prosperity to Puebla than to any other city in New Spain. This wealth revealed itself in the industrialists' mansions and created the city's early façade. Single-family homes inhabited by the bourgeoisie proliferated. These evolved into two-storey structures with rooms built around a patio bordered with passageways —hung with birdcages and decked in flower pots— giving the rooms both ventilation and light. A second patio was used for stables and feedstocks. The

Puebla style in this patio combines wrought iron, plaster, stone, and multicolored talavera tile against an ochre wall.

ground floor was reserved for administrative staff, offices, shops and servants' quarters; the upper floor housed the family. The oratory and the kitchen on the upper floor were central to the household. Most patios had water tanks, some had a fountain.

The *pegostre* technique used by Puebla masons to prepare a high quality sticky mortar appeared in 17th-century houses. Myriad innovations resulted.

Painted white moldings and facings now contrasted with clay brick. Corridors jutted out above the moldings. Arches, refinements and tasteful adornments proliferated. During this time, the region's landlords built homes in the city and created a display of elegance.

Endless style and charm can be found in Puebla doors.

Europe heavily influenced Puebla during the last century. The city welcomed the arrival of the French with their monarchist ideas, as well as the Porfirian relish for overseas imports. After many wars —Independence, Intervention and Reform— that had shrunk production and reduced trade, Puebla experienced a renaissance. Political stability brought modern factories and machinery and spurred industrial growth.

Again, the architecture reflected the renewed prosperity. French and English architects migrated to Puebla to remodel many old buildings in the fashionable neoclassical-style. Some 17th-century homes were so totally renovated that only the foundations were left untouched. The Puebla house continued

to be spacious, but French-style appeared in cornices and abutments, pillars, staircases and adornments. Some patios were even covered with stained glass sunlights. The many public buildings and administrative offices built at this time followed the fashion. This integration of European style gave the city its current distinctive character.

The interiors of the period were splendid. Homes were decorated with chandeliers and mirrors, marble and statuary, giving a grandiose air to the public rooms. Elegant Puebla families lived *à la française*, developing a unique lifestyle which never abandoned its Mexican heritage. Puebla, the quintessential Creole city, is a fine example of cultural hybridization.

Picture yourself ascending a great staircase to be served a cup of chocolate and a tray of colorful sweets ... or enjoying the twice-weekly serenades in the *Zócalo*, attired in the latest fashions.

The Pueblan lives within his own walls, yet he doesn't miss what's happening in the world beyond. While clinging to his traditions, he freely selects from the outside, appropriates what suits him and concocts his own rendition. This is the essence of Puebla style. His home is inhabited, preserved, shared and respected. Its architecture exudes a sense of competence. The houses are much adorned, at times to the point of ostentation; this reflects his urge to confirm his uniqueness. Puebla is a motley collection of contrasting objects, a dislike for "less is more".

Visible manifestations of religiousness abound. There is no house without a cross or without papal benediction; oratories are not unusual in the home. They are dedicated to the Sacred Heart, Saint Michael —the patron saint of Puebla— and the Virgin of Guadalupe. Religion is woven into the fabric of daily life: All Souls Day, baptisms, or processions.

"Pious city! Religious town! This is Puebla de los Angeles!"

My great-grandfather, Sebastián de Mier Almendaro, Mexican Ambassador to France during the Porfirian era, was from Puebla. Partially because of him —or thanks to him— I was born in France. But there came a day when I felt like taking to the road, to follow and find my Puebla roots. I often go to Puebla. I love its architecture and crave its cuisine.

To me, Puebla style is joyful and creative, fanciful, expressive, and daintily adorned. Its distinctive grace borrows freely from others. Puebla style is whimsical. Old-world

Churrigueresque angels of the Capilla del Rosario hold the eagle —symbol of St. John the Evangelist— on walls adorned with gilded plaster and wood figures.

32

romanticism has blended with the ingenious nature of its people, creating a rich tapestry.

Puebla style is to sit in a gold and marble-paneled parlor, where Baccarat chandeliers glow in mirrors brought from Belgium. It is the cascade of a French-style fountain in the colonial patio of an old flour mill. It is a Santo Tomás marble passageway, the intense blue of lintel and pier setting off the oxide red masonry, the 17th-century wrought-iron balcony. It is Atlixco yellow, Chietla blue and the warm gray of the chiseled cantera stone, flecked with *azulejo* tile. These —the colors of Puebla— become more intense after the rains, as the *talavera* shines, the brick darkens, and the skylights gleam.

Puebla style appears in all its glory during All Souls Day in Huaquechula, when the altars to the dead are adorned with angels and cut paper, votive candles and burning incense, seasonal fruit and the bread-of-the-dead, little jugs, chocolate, soft drinks and tequila.

Puebla is a majestic stone staircase, lace filtering the light, a piano covered with a Manila shawl, crystal candelabra, and an embossed brass lamp with a rose fringe. It is a bicycle equipped with tin drums distributing milk in the streets, and the bright eyes of Cholula children. It is the *Churrigueresque* angels of the Rosario Chapel and the naive angels of Santa María de Tonanzintla.

Puebla is the *Casa de Alfeñique,* its cornice molded like icing on a cake; the *Casa de los Muñecos,* its *azulejo* tiles recounting the Herculean labors; the *Casa de los Cañones,* its facade displaying cannons salvaged from a ship by its captain, who came to live in Puebla. It is the neo-Renaissance dining room, its table laid with an embroidered white cloth and set for the thirteen children of the family. It is Mexican flags stuck to adobe walls or staked in among the succulent leaves of the nopal cactus; it is balconies dressed with palms and patriotic ribbons in Izúcar de Matamoros. It is the sugar mills of El Raboso, Colón, La Galarza and El Rijo. It is the San Nicolás Tolentino stone and brick aqueduct with its tooled arches. It is the ancient forest of organ cacti, pointing skyward in Las Bocas, or in Zapotitlán de las Salinas.

Puebla style is Angeles Mastretta's *Arráncame la Vida,* gossip on the porches, the wit in the Hector Azar Theater. It is the shining *talavera* sun and the turned columns trimmed with *azulejo* in the baroque 18th-century church in San Francisco

The round bedroom in the Cabrera sisters' home on the Reforma has a brass bed and walnut furniture.

34

Acatepec. It is the fireworks display during the national holiday at Calmeca, a Mixtec village of pyrotechnic masters, renowned for their bold spirit and machismo. It is the fresco peacocks on the ceiling of a house on the *Reforma* and a marble column in the middle of a bedroom, topped with a pot of artificial azaleas and roses. It is village women fanning themselves serenely on store benches. It is a baroque patio, trimmed with decorated cornices, it is a San Sebastián in a mortar frame, protecting an open passageway. It is an inn transformed into a neighborhood. It is the La Malinche volcano, whence come the rains.

Puebla style is a 1941 black Cadillac, kept in a magnificent colonial patio and carefully dusted before setting out on each trip. It is crisscrossed gauze curtains tied back with pink silk ribbons. It is the flying dancers of Cuetzalan, the Fifth of May in Puebla, the Atlixcayótl Festival in September. It is the flowering fields of marigolds and bishop's rope during All Hallows Eve. It is the legend of the *China Poblana*, the *Nao de China* and the Marchioness Calderón de la Barca's letters. It is a house with *Art Nouveau* crystal glass windows, engraved with swallows on the streetfront and with butterflies on the patio. It is a city where the birds are canaries. It is *talavera*: brick and *talavera*, *talavera* and brick.

Angels inhabit this city; some are of flesh and blood, some of cantera stone, some —those by the cathedral— are cast of bronze, some made of sugar and some carved in gilded wood. The cherubs weep and the seraphs smile.

Chapel of the San Nicolás Tolentino sugar mill, in Izúcar de Matamoros.

The native house
Tradition in the Countryside

Five thousand years B.C., the cultivation of corn began in the valley of Tehuacán, the cradle of settled Mesoamerican culture. Topography dictated that migrants to the pre-Hispanic city-states of the classic era traverse this valley.

Olmec-Xicalancas, Mixtecs and Popolocas were three of the largest groups that came to dominate the region. Cholula became a great ceremonial center, the junction of various cultures.

God provides for the indigenous home. The family shelter, constructed with regional materials, has preserved ethnic cultural values and ancestral traditions since pre-Hispanic times. The center of the single-room house is the hearth. Climate and geography have created four different building styles: one in the mountains, one in the central valley, and still others in the Mixtec and the Popolocan regions.

Mountains border the State of Veracruz on the east and the State of Hidalgo on the west. The rugged terrain of the north of the State is populated by three indigenous groups: the Otomi, the Nahua and the Totonacs. Their homes are similar: rectangular platforms, generally made of wood, which is plentiful, as the

In the region of Oriental, the indigenous house is made of stone and straw; organ cactus, maguey and nopal cactus hedges serve as fences.

39

area is humid and forested. At times stone or adobe is added. The crate-like structure built of rustic planks rests on four wooden posts. An opening is left for the door and occasionally for a window or a porch. The roof is made of thatch, split cane reeds or traditional Mediterranean tile. In more isolated areas, the roof has a layer of *tejamaníl*, thin strips of wood laid clapboard style. Cheerful wall gardens display cans of flowering plants and a variety of treasured herbal medicines. Birdcalls and flowers brighten daily life with music and color.

The family altar is the soul of this one-room house. Its shelf displays patron saints, ancestral photographs, paper and plastic objects, votive candles and domestic appliances. The room has little more than the family bed, covered by a *sarape*. The little chest where clothing is kept is the home's luxury. Made of fragrant wood, the inside is likely to have a mirror adorned with painted angels and flowers.

In Santiago, in the mountainous region of Cuetzalan, Totonac houses are made of stone or adobe with wood and tile roofs.

The corn is stored in a *zontle* in an indoor corner and is covered with sacks, or bundled with dried corn leaves. The granaries are built outside. These are wooden crates resting above the ground on four posts, and covered in *tejamaníl*, to protect the grain from the rain.

The Mixteca is the arid and poor region which borders the States of Guerrero and Oaxaca. Its inhabitants live in isolated little valleys.

In the entrance of an indigenous home, the altar safeguards the bonds to both ancestors and beliefs. Pre-Hispanic culture, Christianity and departed souls are present in daily life. Families are bonded to the land and attuned to the song of life.

Right: A corn silo —cuescomate— in Calmeca, in the Mixtec zone.

Left: Two examples of mountain homes in Cuetzalan both made of wood; one has a tile roof, the other an asbestos roof.

Right: The weave of a palapa in the Mixtec zone.

Next pages: The poetry of the national holidays in San Nicolás Tolentino: Mexican flags staked into a nopal cactus hedge. Nature's bounty is evident in the accessories of indigenous life: a wooden crib, an ixtle sac, a wall of dried maguey leaves, straw mats.

Early Mixtec communities date back to 600 B.C. when the first settled cultures were established. The region's typical house is a hut made of cane or grass wattle secured with *ixtle*, the natural fiber of the aloe shrub. The huts look like little cages roofed with rice or grass straw. Baskets and sacks hangs under the eaves. The Mixtecs sleep on straw mats; their benches are made of tree trunks. The hearth, made of three stones, is set up in a corner; smoke fumigates the thatch and the breeze ventilates the hut. The grain either hangs from the roof, tied together with corn leaves, or is stored outside in a *cuescomate*, a gigantic pot made of wattle and daub, topped with a sort of straw hat to keep out the rain.

The Mixtec kitchen, where Doña María prepares tamales.

Right: A palm-thatch palapa with reed walls is topped with a clay pot, which adorns and protects the top of the hut.

48

In Mixtec communities, villagers gather to build a wattle and daub hut made of woven palm and reeds for the newlyweds. They also put up a village *palapa*, where they can gather to chat and to quench their thirst near their fields and the laundry site. All the work is done on this patio, which is bordered by organ cactus or a hedge of grasses. The corn is shucked and the palm is processed and woven while the children play and the dogs sleep.

The Mixtecs are a jovial and tranquil people. Though poor, they are hospitable and ready to share a plate of beans, flavored *tamalitos* or freshly-made tortillas with a visitor. The door is always open; it may be made of tin, mattress springs, painted poles, pressed board ...

The Popolocan zone includes the districts of Tecamachalco, Tepeji and Tehuacán. It is also arid and cactus plants abound. This land's geological origin is submarine, which explains the limestone cut into slabs and laid by hand without any mortar.

The Popolocan house is larger than the Mixtec or the Serrana. It has a higher roof, which is pitched and covered with a thatch of wild palm. The smoke hatches are under the tie beams.

"The body attains earth's virtues by sleeping on a straw mat on the floor," say the natives. Their *tecuil* hearth is made of *temanaxtle*, the volcanic rock found in the canyon. They manufacture large *comales*, traditional clay platters used for cooking tortillas. The *cuescomate* is the same as in the Mixtec region.

A rough-hewn limestone house with a thatch roof in Molcaxac.

Right: A Popolocan mesote wood door is more of a symbol than a barrier.

The *temascal* is a round stone bath, reminiscent of a bread oven. The interior is heated with wood and when the stone reaches its maximum temperature, it is sprinkled with water, instantly producing steam. After childbirth, a woman is given this ritual bath, made fragrant with aromatic herbs.

The houses in the small town of Tequistepec look like inverted flowers. The structure is made of *mesote*, the dried organ cactus, to which maguey cactus leaves are sewn with natural fibers.

Left: Dried maguey is ideal insulation in this climate.

The "ears" under the tie beams create smoke hatches for the tecuil.

In the fourth region, the Puebla Valley, the villages are close to the cities of Puebla, Cholula, Calpan, Huaquechula, Atlixco and Tecali. Here the houses are made of adobe or stone, but the construction style varies. In some places, small adobe bricks are dried and then stuck together with the same clay. In others, small stones or pieces of brick are placed in the joints to add strength in a process called *rajuelo*. In still other places, like Calpan, solid walls are made with adobe bricks manufactured in the area.

Time and imagination transform adobe.

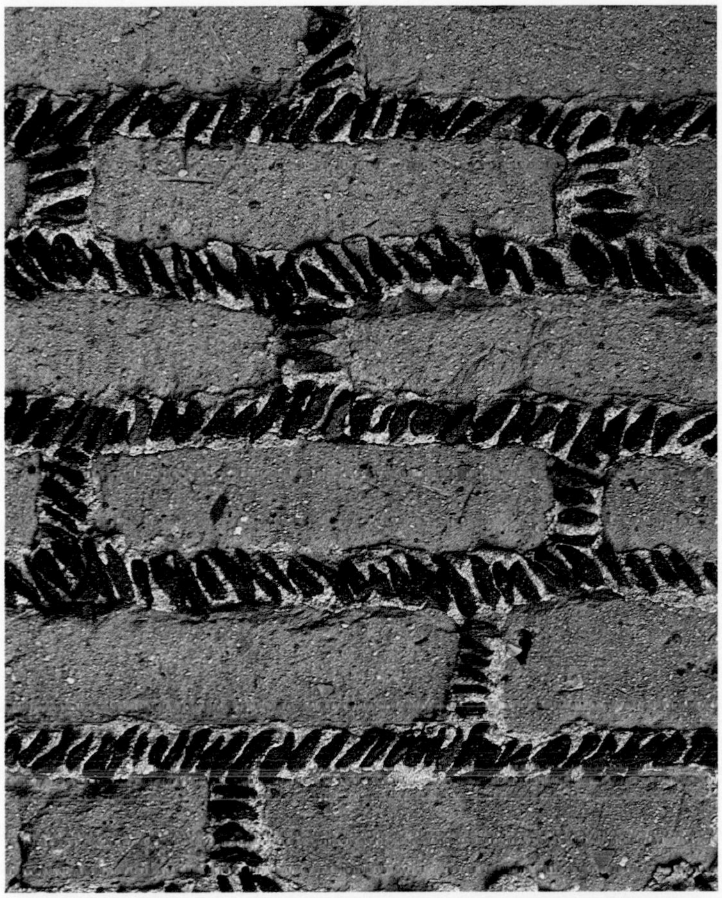
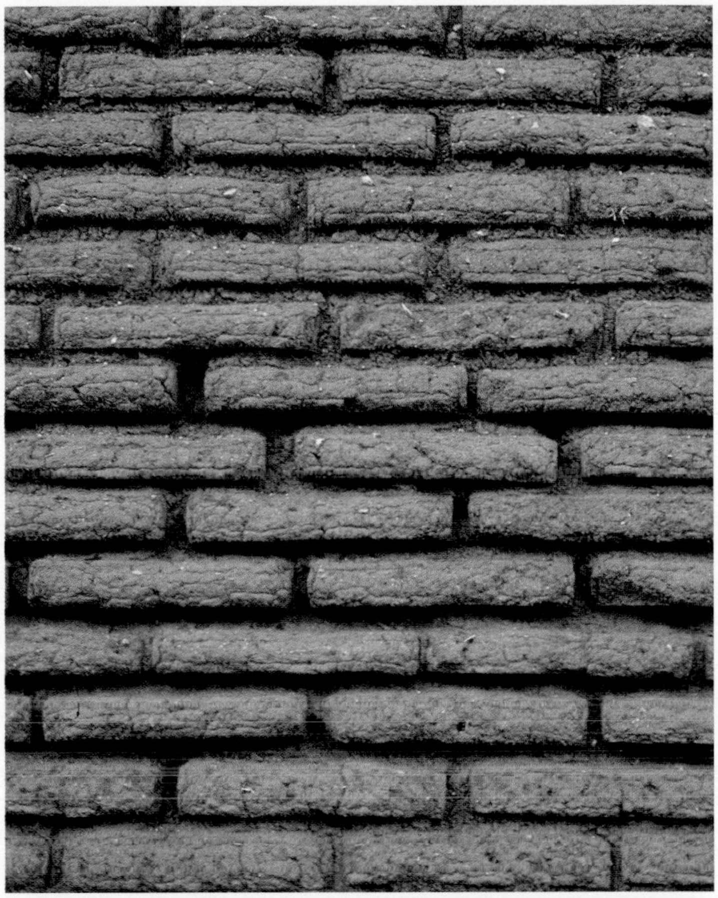
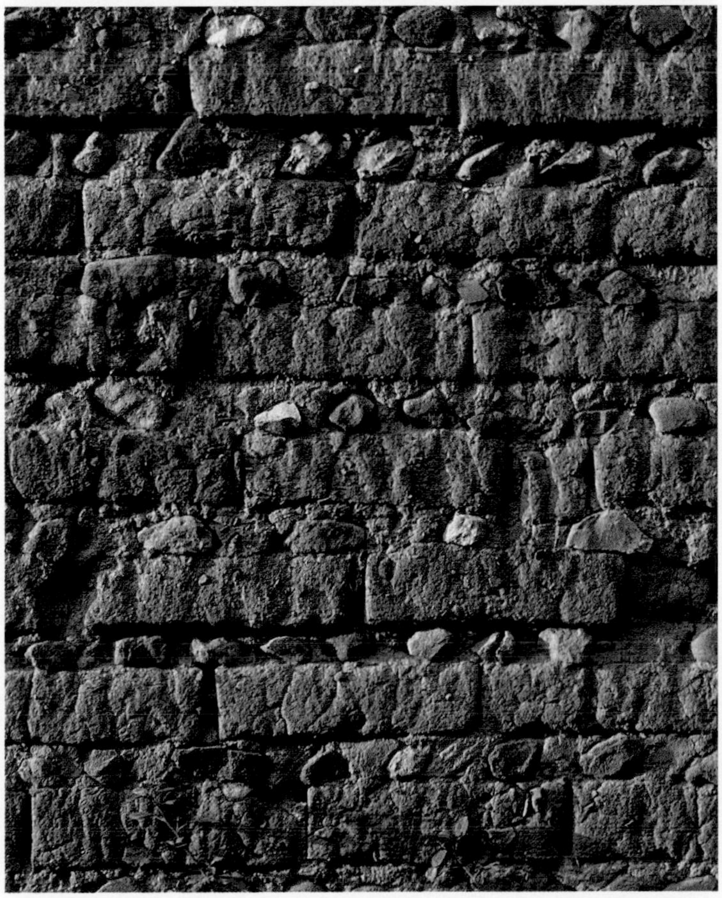
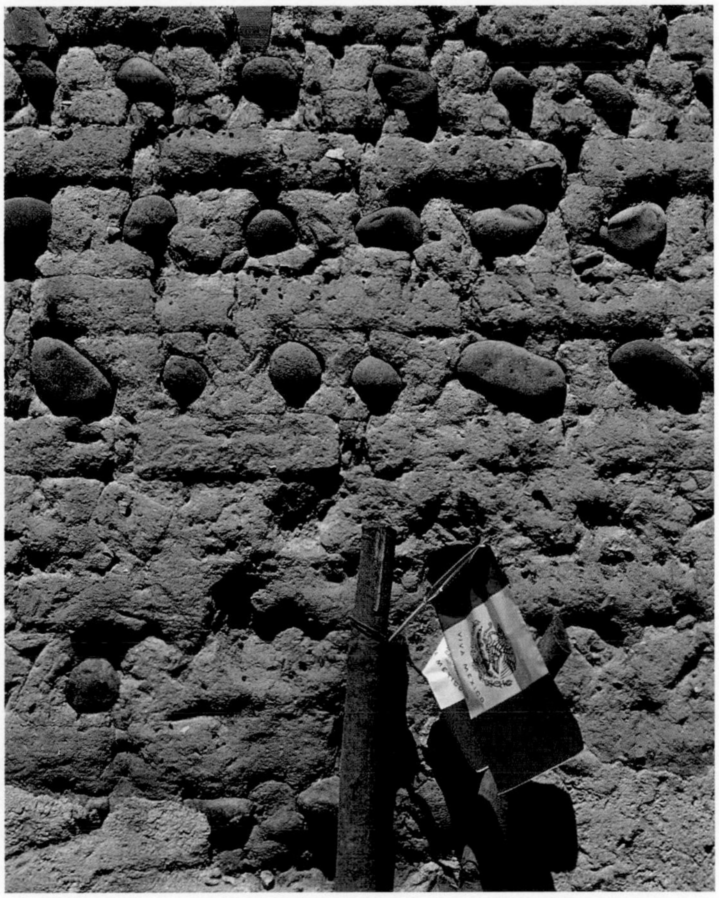

Cholula and Huejotzingo are fertile agricultural areas. Adobe houses with thatch or sheet metal roofs are common. Though one-room homes, the interiors are more furnished. Some have *temascal* baths. In the La Malinche area, the grain is warehoused in granaries. In the vicinities of Cholula, Huejotzingo and Calpan, they use clay silos, called *cencali*, which means the house of the corn.

Patios are part of the farmyard. Chickens cluck among the goats, pigs, ducks, turkeys and the odd goose. Nearby, the family cultivates fruit trees, corn and vegetables. Flowers are one of the main crops of Tonanzintla and Cholula.

Clay on clay in a highland house.

Right: Grain is stored in this cencali in a Cholula yard.

Popular Housing
Typical Mexican Homes

*My talavera tile from Puebla
displays the portraits of my mother,
my girlfriend and my sister.*

—José Reseck Saade

F iesta. The streets dressed in color and laughter await the celebration as Nahuas, Otomis and Totonacs in vivid finery descend like rivers from their mountain homes, into Cuetzalan. It is October the 4th, the *fiesta* of San Francisco in Cuetzalan, the festival of coffee and the festival of the *huipil*.

Pre-Hispanic and Spanish roots commemorate the *quetzal* and its colored plumage. The balconies of the cobblestone streets leading to the town square are decorated and the church is dressed with flowers and rosettes fashioned with the hearts of the palm fronds. History is reenacted as pagans and Christians dance the *Santiago* midst a commotion of disguise and capes. The town transforms itself into a world of masked dreams.

The energy of anticipation is in the air; children run, street vendors bustle merchandise about and the traditional ballet, the *Baile de los Negritos* is set up. *La Mainguilla*, an adolescent dressed as a maiden, will play *La Malinche*. Hats are distributed among the booths, lady vendors wear *quezquémil* blouses trimmed with colored ribbons at the neckline and ties plaited into their hair. The men retire for a glass of *yolispa*, the regional beverage made of sixteen aromatic herbs. The *Quetzalines* begin to band together and to tune their instruments.

Hearts of palm rosettes and wild orchids decorate a traditional festival.

61

The flyers arrive in Cuetzalan; they are the best dancers from Totonacapan, jealous guardians of this religious and astrological tradition. Their leader leads them up the staff. The anticipation peaks in that instant when the dancers throw themselves to the four winds from the perch at the top, with the same élan that their ancestors once exhibited. Legend holds that they flew forever.

The *fiesta*—color and music to intoxicate the senses— is an old custom. September is the month of the Atlixcayótl, the festival of the indigenous dances in Atlixco. In a show of pride, dance groups from all the regions honor the village that gave them life.

On national holidays in Izúcar de Matamoros, balconies are decorated with palms, ribbons and little flags. On September the fifteenth, there are Mariachis, a great "Viva México!" and a castle of pyrotechnic lights from Calmeca. *Tostadas* also go patriotic with the green, white and red of lettuce, onions and tomatoes.

Quetzal children —already flying dancers— walk along the streets of Cuetzalan on the feast day of San Francisco.

Right: Nahuatl women on their way to the huipil contest.

Huaquechula welcomes everyone to its Feast of the Dead. Traditional 'bread of the dead' and a mug of chocolate is offered to all visitors. The white altars are feminine, typically Puebla. Four altar levels covered in satin, tulle and lace display little angels, votive candles and incense; marigolds and paper and plastic flowers reach to the ceiling. If the death is recent, a path of flower petals links the altar to the graveyard.

Mole, cookies, and little jugs surround Doña Elvira Castro's portrait. It seems that the magnificence of the altar-piece reflects the esteem given to the deceased; family and friends, godchildren and godparents come to light a candle and to sing the departed soul's favorite verses. Families work all year long to create a fitting altar. The Feast of the Dead commemorates life.

A cart, brimful of marigolds, heads for the Day of the Dead festivities.

Right: Day of the Dead altar beneath a Christ made of corn leaves. Cuautinchán convent.

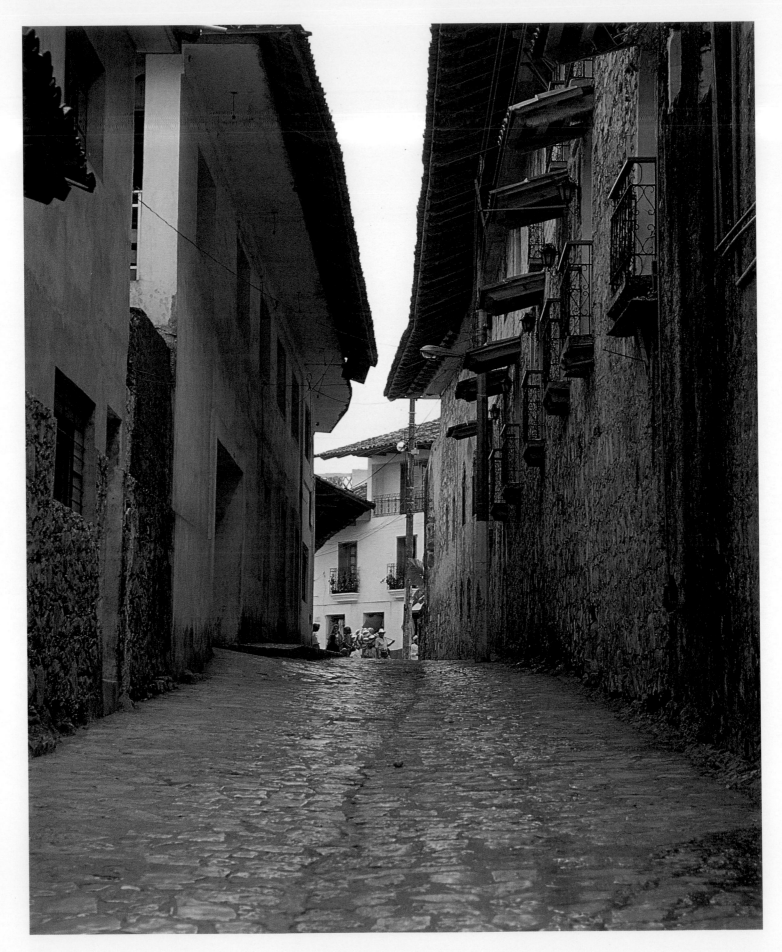

Popular housing is guileless. Created without design nor plans, it grows along with the family needs. Rooms are added here and there, as wealth permits. The house is never finished but is constantly altered, as it echoes every man's customs. Everything inside is sensible and flexible; a shop banquette can serve as a bench or to display merchandise, or to dispense fruit beverages.

As the house undergoes its transformation, unusual building solutions produce nooks and recesses and sensible staircases. The resulting style goes beyond poverty and ingenuity; it adds poetry to the practical, dignity to simplicity.

Popular housing deals with the absence of rules. Color is for enjoyment. A sense of humor makes a kaleidoscope of the little streets. Spontaneity produces correct proportions. Houses are coquettish, display and adornment being important. One may be trimmed with flowers, another filled with pots or canary cages, while still another can boast a shade tree in the patio.

Left: Roofs almost touch in a street in Cuetzalan.

The lightheartedness of the people of Cuetzalan is visible in their houses.

*Left: Mexican decor in a
17th-century home in Huejotzingo.*

*A window in Santiago
Yancuitlalpan.*

*The simplicity of pastel colors
prevails in Zacapoaxtla.*

Good materials transformed by skilled craftsmen stamp the house with authenticity. In Cuetzalan, the ground floor of the mountain home is made of stone while the upper floor has balconies and wooden tiles. In Zacapoaxtla, the winged eaves protect the pedestrian from the rains. Dust-guards are painted ochre, blue or pink. The streets are a colorful scene as donkeys and merchants, children and townfolk come and go to or from the market, hither and thither.

Wooden balconies and jutting eaves are characteristic of Zacapoaxtla architecture.

Right: Daily life in the streets of Cuetzalan.

Next pages: Skirting protects façades in damp climates. Zacapoaxtla.

Each district of the city of Puebla has its own crafts. Xanenetla is known for its *xalnene* stone flower pots. Xonaca makes jugs and pitchers and the Barrio de la Luz produces dinnerware, *pulque* jugs and *mole* pots in ovens that can date back to the 16th century. The artisans live and work in nearby houses. In this same district they manufacture the pressed glass used to make the large *pulque* mug and a variety of different glasses used for specific drinks.

Popular ingenuity has transformed daily life. On the Paseo Bravo, a bench mosaic of painted *azulejo* tile depicts the *China Poblana* in the arms of a *charro*. The forms multiply and metamorphose, each mosaic forming a flower or a star. The spontaneous and bold use of color —to be found in an unusual trim, or a painted window frame— titillates the pedestrian's eye.

The streets of Huejotzingo are a series of whites, greens, lilacs and yellows. Behind the 16th-century Franciscan convent, in front of an aqueduct, there is a pretty home with a scalloped Mudéjar arch leading to a garden framed in vivid hues.

In Huaquechula, a window's curved balconies become a novel, a story of past squabbles. In Cholula, tile lines roofs and porches and crowns the walls; the clay tile is shaped by the same hands that work in the nearby fields.

Crossing the threshold of the popular dwelling brings a surprise. Doña Chole invites us into her living room. Decorated with deluxe curtains, its table is covered with a plastic lace cloth, ceramic figures and photographs of her grandparents' wedding. A bright bedspread, large wardrobe and mirror set off the bedroom. Doña Chole offers us *tamales* and *atole* in the kitchen, where women chat, help children with their homework or make candelabra and dolls for the altar of the dead.

Doña Amalia still uses steel irons, the kind that are filled with hot coals. "An electric iron? What use is it if the lights are always going out?"

Firewood stacked against the walls under the eaves of highland homes.

Over the years, once-grand Puebla city homes have been converted into *vecindades*, multi-family dwellings. Each one has a patron saint and its *fiesta*. It is an extended family, bonds and feuds and all. An open gate reveals this world of doors, stairs and windows, clothes hanging on the line, dogs and children playing beneath the paper garlands of the last fiesta. The comedy, the eternal theater of life, plays out beneath old railings among the pots and the gossip. The patio is the lifeline of the families joined in a secret pact, sharing joys and sorrows and protecting one another.

Juan from unit "A" leaves at six to deliver newspapers on his bicycle, while his wife prepares a meal for the children who are rinsing their faces in the washbasin before going to school. Don José from unit "C" is a carpenter; he takes his tools out to the patio. Next door Doña Chona, his good friend, is making the *tamales* that she will sell at the gate. They are all busy; next month they have to deliver the Judases for the *Fiesta* of Holy Saturday.

A door guards the privacy of each home. In Puebla, it can be made of wood, laminated metal, or ironwork. It can be simple, or trimmed with a sculpted relief, or adorned with big steel nails. It can have a peephole for spying outsiders or it can have a little door, just for the eyes. One is tempted to look in! Some have doorbells, others have shiny knockers, variously shaped. They open and close continually. Puebla doors are an invitation to enter, to discover the mysteries that they hide.

Puebla Cuisine
Kitchens and Customs

Hey! San Pascual Bailón!
You spring and dance and almost fly
Midst the pots and the pans ...
Season my pipián!
Blessed San Pascual, hear my plea,
I offer you my prayer with a soaring heart.
Put some love into my pot!

—*Popular Refrain*

N uns' hands chop the onion, tomato and parsley, the candied lemon, plums, pears, peaches, raisins and almonds; they pull apart the pork meat into threads, peel the nuts, add the peanuts, cloves and cinnamon, shucking their rosaries as scarlet drops gush from the pomegranate.

Twenty four ingredients went into the tricolored *chiles en nogada* when the dish was first made during Independence —in the Santa Mónica Convent— to celebrate Don Agustín de Iturbe's feast day, after the Treaty of Cordoba.

The nuns scurry around the *anafre* stove in the middle of the kitchen, midst pots and simmering aromas. Their gardens grow Spanish condiments and vegetables, unknown in local markets.

Other genteel, creative nuns —in the Santa Rosa Convent— cheerfully spend time under the 17th-century tiled vaults of their kitchen. They work at the *anafre* stove, at the mortars —grinding chocolate and mole— and at the *comal,* cooking the *tortillas.* To welcome the Viceroy, they invented the delicacy that blends Indian and Spanish traditions, the now famous *mole poblano.*

The Santa Clara nuns brought Puebla a sweet trip through Spain and the Arab world as their baroque imagination shaped

Chiles en nogada served on a talavera platter.

frivolities with almonds and sugar: *camotes, jamoncillos, gorditas, rosquillas, charamuscas, trompadas, polvorones, mazapanes, muéganos* and *alfajores*. They also made an eggnog liqueur called *rompope*. They added some pre-Hispanic mementos to this selection with *alegrías* and *palanquetas*. To this day, along the convent street there are sweet shops with counters covered in colored cut paper and sugar figurines.

Hanging tamaleras in the San Bernardino ranch.

Right: A Totonac great-grandmother stirs the beans in the kitchen.

To make *mole poblano*, you start at the market. Every town has a fixed market day. In Tepeaca, where Hernán Cortés had a home, it is on Friday; in Atlixco and Huejotzingo, on Saturdays; in Puebla on Tuesdays and Thursdays. Regional produce and articles are sold: domestic appliances, straw mats, chairs and baskets; fruit and vegetables; clothing and crafts.

Sweet chilies are from San Martín, hot ones from Miahuatlán, walnuts come from Huejotzingo, apples from Zacatlán, pomegranates from Tehuacán and the pork is from Cholula. The chili *atole* and *chalupas* are from Paseo Viejo and the bread from Tecamachalco. *Tejocote* fruit comes from San Salvador el Verde, peanuts from the Mixtec region, prickly pears from Zapotitlán, *pitahaya* fruit from San José, *yolispa* liquor from Cuetzalan, the sugar cane aquavit called *guaro* from Izúcar de Matamoros, and the flowers from Atlixco. And to carry it all away in, there will be baskets from Ajalpan. Special products appear during festivals and patron saint celebrations. In some more isolated towns, a traditional form of barter still exists.

Major regional fiestas include the San Francisco fiesta in Cuetzalan, that of San Miguel —celebrating the famous carnival in Huejotzingo— and that of San Francisco Apetlahuacan, where the State of Puebla's native dance festival is held.

An outdoor Mixtec kitchen, next to the bread oven and the granary.

Right: Jugs, jars, pots and mortars all have a place in the Puebla kitchen.

Puebla has particular recipes to honor special occasions. During Lent, there are twelve soup stews, stuffed *chipotle* chilies, shrimp, potato and rice pancakes, cauliflower and *huauzontles*, and a dish made with greens and dried fish called *verdolagas*. During Holy Week, there's *muégano* and little ring rolls. During Corpus Christi, the specialty is green or red *pipián*. The Feast of the Dead is celebrated with puff pastry cut-outs, *chimisclán*, *nicoatole* and *manchamanteles*, a chicken and fruit stew. *Tamalitos*, *barbacoa*, fried tortillas, breads and sweets also appear on the altars.

Hacienda and city mansion kitchens were often gigantic. During the fiestas, they served banquets to hundreds of people. Almost all have conserved their *anafre* ovens and some still have bread-making ovens. The walls are covered with clay pots of all sizes and *talavera* tile shelves, where the fruit paste was cooled in great copper pots.

The kitchen is in the geographic center of the Santa Mónica Convent. The free-standing stove allows the nuns to transit freely into the refectory. On the walls and in recesses: jars, jugs, pots and wine bottles. Don Agustín de Iturbide first tasted chiles en nogada created in this kitchen.

Right: The kitchen of the 17th-century Santa Rosa convent is lined with talavera. Convent life combined hospitality and creativity, which resulted in the exquisite cuisine of Puebla. The famous mole poblano was invented here, at the instigation of Bishop Manuel Fernández de la Cruz, circa 1680.

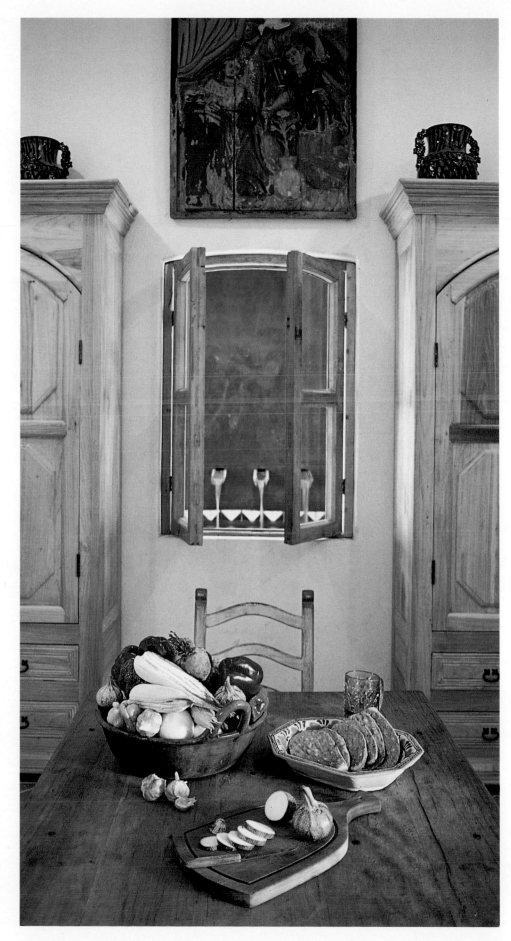

Left: A detail in the Casa de Alfeñique kitchen. Above the sideboard, where the dinnerware is stored, wooden shelving displays Puebla talavera pottery.

Right: The San José Munive kitchen looks out over an indigo blue fountain.
The wooden furniture is designed in the ex-hacienda by Esteban Chapital.

Next Pages: Four 19th-century still-life paintings by the popular painter Agustín Arrieta. (Private collections. Photographs by Bob Schalkwijk.)

In the Indian house, the kitchen centers around the *tecuil* hearth, where an enormous clay pan —from Reyes Mezontla— is heated. Next to it stands a jug of fruit beverage and the *nixtamal* pot for the corn dough to be converted into *tortillas*. There is also a stack of pots for making the *mole,* the rice, the beans and the *atoles,* a cornmeal drink. The walls are hung with jugs, pots and pans, wooden spoons and much love. There is always a stove for the *tamales*, the chili *atole*, and for the beans, to be refried with herbs and cactus.

The sinks in the Santa Rosa convent are made of Chiluca stone and decorated with talavera tiles.

Right: A pot from the Barrio de la Luz sits on a stove burner in the Casa de Alfeñique.
Talavera combines geometry and color in the Santa Rosa convent kitchen.

Puebla style travels to a country kitchen in Tepoztlán, in the State of Morelos.

To come to the table in Puebla is a ritual. It is the ceremony of the family reunion and a soapbox for harangues against one's neighbor. It is Mother's domain. With great talent and skill, she eagerly seasons, contrasts, mixes and adorns subtle ingredients, colors and flavors, creating sublime pleasure. Kitchens, kaleidoscopes of delicious sensations, are made of brick, stone, tile plaster and wrought iron.

The towns of Puebla State bake a variety of breads for the many festivals and holidays; these can be seasoned with almonds, sesame seeds, chilies, anise, cinnamon, nuts or even squash seeds.

Like bread, Puebla dishes are shared. A Mexican kitchen is never without *talavera*, green glass or clay pots from the Barrio de la Luz. And there will never be a fiesta without *mole*.

A riot of Puebla color finds a home in Güera Gomez' Mexico City cupboard.

The Haciendas
Plantations, Ranches and Farms

T he air smells of the sweet fragrance of honey from the smoke of the burning husks rising from the furnace. Ranch hands prepare the carriages and harness the oxen, as stewards and overseers call out the orders to the workers in the El Raboso sugar mill patio.

Don Antonio Raboso y de la Plaza canters up on his chestnut horse, returning all sweaty and dusty from his tour of the burning reed-beds. Doña Lupe runs out of the house with a decanter of fresh water. The priest of the Santo Domingo parish alights from his buggy. All is ready for the benediction mass to be celebrated at the start of the sugar cane harvest.

The great mill wheel starts to turn slowly as the spillway gate of the aqueduct is opened. The workers recite their prayers in chorus. The work will go on day and night —without a break— for fifteen weeks, until the breads, the sugar loafs, the treacle and the spirits have all been processed.

Four months later, Doña Cristina welcomes her husband to their mansion home on the Calle 4 Oriente, in Puebla. Knowing that the harvest has been successful, she has agreed to finance an altar piece for the San Nicolás Cathedral as well as a silver lamp and San Liborio Obispo canvas. She also considers covering the dome of her own chapel with tile and embellishing her balconies with stucco sculptures. Prosperity is in the air.

The granary of the San José Zacatepec hacienda supplied the wheat to 16th-century New Spain. The colonial sense of space provided inspiration to Architect Luis Barragán and other contemporary Mexican architects.

The *hacienda* —legacy of the Spanish rule which granted grandees land for agricultural or livestock exploitation— was a self-sufficient production center. *Haciendas* came to include pens for draught animals, corrals, stables and barns as well as water cisterns, grain silos and pastures for the livestock. Employees lived in adobe hamlets just outside the *hacienda*.

The chapel was the soul of the *hacienda*, where the Patron Saint was honored, and religious rites and community meetings were held. Adjacent facilities and barns were built to provide for the principal crop and manufacturing needs. The landlord's house was almost always a two-storey structure; the ground floor housed the offices, the overseer's quarters, the *hacienda* store, the saddle maker and the storerooms. The upstairs was reserved for the formal salon and dining room, the bedrooms, the kitchen and a workroom, where preserves, cheeses and sausages were made.

The 16th-century El Raboso sugar mill, near Izúcar de Matamoros. The neoclassical chapel was half destroyed during the Revolution.

Foot of the stairs and balustrade at the wheat mill at Huexotitla, on the San Francisco river bank. 19th century

Right: French-style dining room in the Huexotitla mill house; 19th century.

Next pages: The garden of the San Cristóbal Polaxtla hacienda is Porfirian-style, with its marble bridge and 19th-century French romantic sculptures. Don Antonio Haghenbeck transformed the old Jesuit hacienda into a country home.

Left: An English-style castle, built by Bishop Gillow, stands at the edge of the lake in the Chautla hacienda garden.

Right: View of the 17th-century aqueduct arcade, which brought the water to the Chautla mill wheel.

Partial view of the entrance to the Chautla hacienda mill.

Near the entrance to the Tamariz hacienda is the saddle room, used by the overseers and the cowboys.

The head groom has played an important role in the life of the cattle haciendas since the time of the conquest.

Next pages: Monumental entrance to the main patio at the Tamariz hacienda.

Tamariz was one of the most important cattle haciendas since Viceregency times. In the stable, cut stone pilasters support the Catalan-style brick vaults.

They say that *charrería* —which became the rodeo— began in the state of Puebla during the time of the viceroys, when Blessed Sebastián de Aparicio introduced horsemanship to the native peoples, teaching them to use the rope, throw the bull by the tail and wrangle and break in horses. The large *hacienda* ranches of the time produced milk, meat and jerky, soap and tallow, and leather for saddle making. To this day, the Ozumba area has ranches with thousands of head of cattle, with milking and breeding facilities, corrals and stables and pens that look like stockyards. Cowboys, overseers and ranch hands live in a wing off the central house.

Hacienda homes were restored during the Porfirian era, at the turn of the century, to achieve the look of English castles. The grain was stored in giant barns, built by the Jesuits over the years when the church —through guilds and stewardships— came to administer two thirds of all the *hacienda*s and ranches.

119

Left: The interior façade of the central patio at Tamariz is richly adorned with Italian-style romantic frescos.

Right: The stable —where draught animals were kept— is the oldest part of Tamariz, which dates back to the 17th century.

A flight of steps separates the patio from the backyard. Tamariz hacienda.

A happy party in carriages, coaches and buggies is escorted by a fine Mariachi band, as it travels a dirt road to attend the wedding of a rancher's eldest son. He is on his way to marry his neighbor's daughter; the properties will stay in the family.

San Antonio Polaxtla's greatest prosperity came after the French intervention and still keeps Napoleonic memories. During the Porfirian years, its colonial *hacienda* was transformed into a romantic European palace.

The chapel and stables of the San José Ozumba hacienda.

Next pages: Built in the fortress-style —with turrets and battlements— the San José Ozumba hacienda was remodeled at the end of the 19th century by Architect Tamariz.

When the *hacienda*s were dispossessed of their lands during the Revolution, many were left abandoned. Removal or loss of their valuable furnishings left country homes austere when agricultural production ceased. Today, the interiors of these once-grand homes —like San Antonio de Virreyes— have an almost monastic simplicity. Some still use gas lamps and burn wood in the bread ovens and *anafres*, as they await an occasional visit from proprietors, drawn back by nostalgia and the need to supervise the property.

Left: Vestiges of the El Rijo sugar mill aqueduct.

The two-storey arcade of the mill in Bishop Gillow's hacienda.

Esteban and Lidia Chapital have restored the former grain producing *ex-hacienda* of San José Munive on the Huejotzingo highway, near San Andrés Chautla, previously remodeled by Bishop Gillow. The Chapitals design and manufacture traditional hand crafted Puebla furniture for country homes and modern houses. Colonial treasures and Sebastián abstract sculptures fill the spacious patios. The billiard room is dedicated to Colunga; the great salon is dedicated to Felguérez. San José Munive transcends time; the walls preserve their ancestral beauty and this energy is transformed into contemporary creativity.

Sebastián sculpture stands out against the whitewashed walls of the San José Munive hacienda.

Inside the San José Munive hacienda: the game room, dedicated to painter Alejandro Colunga.

An indigo blue drinking trough and stone fountain with a tile rim.

Next pages: Large-scale dining room furniture, designed by Esteban Chapital.

Detail of the salon dedicated to painter Manuel Felguérez.

131

The Viceregency
16th-Century Architecture

There are angels everywhere in Puebla. This one is in the frieze that frames the murals in the Casa del Deán. The seraph wears a pre-Hispanic pectoral medallion.

The ideal spot on which to build the first Spanish city, called Cuitlaxcoapan by the Nahua people, lay in the Loreto and Guadalupe foothills, between the San Francisco and Atoyac rivers. On one side of the valley rose the mighty profile of the La Malinche volcano, and on the other the Popocatépetl and the Iztaccíhuatl.

Alonso Martín de Ovando had requested royal permission to build a new settlement to provide a center and a refuge for the Spaniards. On January 18, 1531, Juan Salmerón brought the royal approval. Brother Toribio de Motolinía celebrated the first mass on the site soon to become Puebla. The founders, following the angels' design according to Julian Garcés' dream, began to create a Renaissance utopia. The prize properties near the main square were distributed to the conquistadors. The privileges guaranteed by royal decree were of great interest to the minor noblemen, soldiers and adventurers eager to make their fortunes through hard work. The number of the first group of settlers (thirty three families originating from Extremadura, Galicia and Andalusia), was thought to be a propitious reference to Christ's age when he died.

Their first dwellings, built with adobe and straw, were gradually substituted by massive stone fortresses that served as places of work, factories, stores and housing. Settlers came from Atlixco, Calpan, Huejotzingo, Cholula, Huaquechula and Tepeaca. Puebla had over three hundred Spanish families by 1549 and introduced potable water in 1557. This growth attracted the finest artisans of the time; their crockery and glass was soon exported to Guatemala. Master artisans from Flanders and Greece arrived to establish wrought iron workshops and install the first looms, in this city destined to be a leading industrial center.

In early Puebla houses —those of the first decade— walls prevail over openings.

Life in 16th-century Puebla was austere and dominated by religion. Brotherhoods and chaplaincies were created to support the guilds and thanks to the efforts of the pious, many convents were built. An evangelizing euphoria reigned.

The predominating architectural styles were Renaissance —with some Gothic touches— and Plateresque, named for its similarity to the embossed silver work. Period pillars, columns and cornices feature classical Greco-Roman art forms; Arabic influence is evident in the ironwork, the patios and the water tanks.

Spanish buildings were designed to protect the people and their goods. The mild climate allowed for open patios, which were cheerful and healthy spaces. The house of the time is low, with far more wall than windows and doors. The wooden windows are trimmed with grilles and the small rooms get little light. Sunlit patios have robust Tuscan-style columns in their passages. The builders used thick, solid supporting walls to strengthen the structure against earthquakes. They adapted new materials to build flat roofs without rail work, and beamed brick ceilings. In

The passage of the centuries has left few 16th-century buildings intact. The San José parish has a classic Renaissance entrance made of cut stone.

137

In front of San Agustín, the *Casa de las Cabecitas* has two Renaissance medallions with two busts over its front entrance. Its classical stone porch is of monumental proportions. From the time it was built until today, it remains a rooming house patio.

Right: The great stonemasons came from Huaquechula. They were trained in the use of tools by Fray Martín de Valencia. Saint Martin, on the front of the Huaquechula convent.

One of New Spain's greatest 16th-century artworks is the *Casa del Deán*, which originally belonged to Don Tomás de la Plaza, the Cathedral deacon in charge of the church treasury. The 1580 Renaissance façade has an entrance flanked by Doric columns and topped with a balcony adorned with Ionic pillars, believed to have been sculpted by Juan de Alcántara. The Italian-style frescos adorning the main rooms depict classic alegories, religious symbols and scenes from life at court. The first room shows the world of the redemption as announced by the sibyls, prophets on horseback bearing standards. The frieze, edged with stripes and plant designs, monkeys and flowers, is reminiscent of the pre-Hispanic *codices*. It is a charming world of cherubs, deer and birds. The second room shows the triumphs of death, love, purity and fame. Each work has a symbol and the *Grutesco* frames are adorned with maidens, plumes and crests.

Façade of the Casa del Deán.

Right and next pages: These unique 16th-century murals in the Casa del Deán combine Italian Renaissance with a pre-Hispanic legacy.

In 1572 English merchants arrived in Puebla in search of *cochinilla, añil,* honey, silk and pottery to take to Europe. One of them, John Chiton, described with admiration the beauty of the great valley and the elegance of the city.

A beautiful 16th-century Cholula house displays carved eagle knights —pre-Hispanic warriors— on the piers of its façade, a most unusual adornment for a Spanish house. The *Casas Reales* —built to house the governors and other city officials— still stand in Atlixco's main square, exhibiting the crests of the early grandees on their façade and Tuscan-style columns in the porticos.

Public buildings of the period still exist in Puebla: the arches in the *Zócalo,* under which Spanish goods could be bought. On market days —Tuesdays and Thursdays— Indians from the neighboring villages would sell their produce there. In Tepeaca, the *Rollo* —where delinquents were punished and the laws of trade were agreed— still exists. The house which once belonged to Hernán Cortés was totally remodeled during the 17th and 18th centuries.

Puebla's religious architecture of the 16th century is splendid. Convent styles vary from fortress with battlements to Elizabethan Gothic, to Renaissance. In the Tecali convent, the classical proportions are majestic, the ceilings wainscoted, and the walls adorned with frescos. The gigantic water cistern, which helped them get through the droughts, has also been conserved, as well as the patio of the orange trees, and the famed baptismal font sculpted in Gothic motifs. Cuauntinchán rises out of the landscape like a fortress built on the platform of a pre-Hispanic temple. Huejotzingo is known for the beauty of its chapels and bells —which respond to one another— and the Plateresque altarpieces painted by Juan de la Concha.

Eagle warrior in the spandrel of a Cholula door.

Right: Porticos and Casas Reales —royal houses— in the main square of Cholula and Atlixco.

The Viceregency
17th-Century Architecture

A celestial scene: angels attending court as guests.

On April 18, 1649 the Spanish King's envoys, governors, officials and visitors all met to render homage to his Excellency Bishop Juan de Palafox y Mendoza, during the consecration of the Puebla Cathedral. The bishop was given a gold key engraved with the Royal Coat of Arms in recognition of his efforts to finish the construction. One thousand five hundred workers and officials participated in the building.

The inauguration was a memorable event. The passage from the Kings' altar to the atrium was carpeted; the guilds competed for the right to adorn the Cathedral chapels. The inaugural procession made a dazzling entrance under a red velvet canopy to the music of trumpets and choirs. The city's founding families attended, resplendent in their brocades, laces and pearls. Standard poles, canopy holders, great candelabra and the one meter square tabernacle were all made of chiseled silver. For many years, people spoke of the opulent celebration and of its great cost.

There were jousts in the main square. Bullfights. A procession escorted by giant allegorical floats. A masquerade ball was put on by the ninety-eight grandees who came dressed as the Kings of Spain, from early Gothic princes to those of the mighty Austrian dynasty. During the nine days of celebrations, there were daily flower exhibitions and nightly fireworks.

Elegant Tuscan-style column in a patio across the street from the Cathedral.

In Puebla, the 17th century is a religious time; it is the Palafox era. Various fraternities are hard at work creating guilds, financing pious works and building convents. The convents of Santa Catarina, San Jeronimo and La Concepción are joined by Santa Teresa, Santa Clara, La Santísima, Santa Inés, Santa Mónica and Santa Rosa.

Bishop Juan de Palafox y Mendoza came to New Spain to be the bishop of Puebla and to do an audit for the Viceroy. His dynamism and leadership made him famous. He founded the secular seminary, the San Juan and San Pedro colleges, and the library that bears his name. To this day, its shelves contain important volumes —not only religious works— dealing with the sciences, medicine, architecture and astrology. The collection, organized by themes, is sensitive to the humanities. The seminary was an institution of higher learning, where they taught indigenous languages, so useful for evangelization. In 1640, the first printing press was established in Puebla.

The Palafox Library in the seminary founded by Don Juan de Palafox y Mendoza in the 17th century has fifty thousand books. To this day, it is the best-conserved Viceregnum library in Latin America.

Right: The Cathedral is one of religious art's most important creations. It was built almost entirely in the 17th century in the Mannerist-style. Its interior was remodeled in the neoclassical-style in the 19th century by the Architect Manzo.

The city's fame spreads throughout the kingdom. By 1678, there are 70,000 inhabitants. In Puebla, city of domes and cloisters, the tolling of the bells blends with the pounding of the hammers and the murmuring looms.

"The factories employing the brethren (owned, with good reason, by the most skilled) produce delicate fabrics such as wool and Chinese cotton, flawless crockery, finer pottery than that of Talavera, crystal and glass, a variety of choice weapons and fireworks that are famous throughout the Kingdom for their refined temper and excellent craftsmanship. But among all of these factories, the richest, most abundant and opulent is the soap factory, which supplies the entire Kingdom. Other workshops and factories produce such quality that with good reason can Puebla be called the Barcelona of America ..."

Puebla's peak coincides with that of the great silver production. New Spain's wealth increases manufacturing demand. Mills, meat producers, textile plants, tanners, saddlers, candlemakers and glassmakers take orders from all the provinces and export to Guatemala and Peru. The quality of the cotton cloth, tallow, glass and tiles is exceptional. Wrought iron workers, plasterers, and stone hewers compete with carpenters, cabinet makers and painters. The first architects and master-architects establish themselves. Artists specialize in silver, furniture and religious paintings.

By royal decree every *hacendado* must own a house in the city; Puebla, the Spanish city *par excellence,* attracts *hacendados* from everywhere —from the Veracruz coast to Acapulco— to build their mansions in the City of the Angels.

As protection against the frequent floods, buildings were lined with a stone skirting; the brick and tile walls were then covered with either plaster or quarry stone. Puebla's unique physiognomy was being born; baroque abandoned the straight line in favor of the curve; adornment and contrast were popular. The *Grustesco* and the *Churrigeresque* appeared, with iron brackets, crests, masks, cornices, railings, turned columns and *estípite* pilasters. Houses became taller and slimmer, with roof railings, fancy grillwork and rosettes on the doors. Pueblans used their patios as a workplace, and not as a living space like the Andalusians. In Puebla, people are invited into a salon; the patio is only used when the size of the banquet requires it.

Dome of the La Concepción convent.

Next pages: Chinese art influences Puebla tile in the Santa Rosa convent.

Brick and talavera give Puebla façades both color and personality.

154

155

158

Left: Built by a ship captain, the Casa de los Cañones, on the old road to Cholula, is named for the cannons that adorn its façade. The rich detail of the wrought iron in the long balcony is evidence of the skill of the artisans.

Tile and cornices are used to highlight and to distinguish the façades of 17th-century architecture. A Prelate's residence on the corner of 4 Sur and 3 Oriente.

162

The Pinacoteca Museum, built by
Puebla's official architect, Diego
de la Sierra, served as the Jesuit
residence. It was previously called
Casa de la Bóveda (House of the
Dome) and Casa del Canon Peláez
(House of the Canon Peláez).
The Andalusian patio which
features curves —either in plaster
or carved stone— is adorned with a
central fountain lined with tiles
reminiscent of the Mudéjar style.

The stairwell has an Arab-style
double arch. A statue of Saint
Ignatius sits in a recess; an onyx
dome softens the light. In the
foreground: Corinthian
fluted-stone columns.

163

The Viceregency
18th-Century Architecture

M idst fluttering fans and revelry, the candelabra were lit and fine silk gloves grazed the railings of the theater boxes. Nobody could pass up the inauguration of the first real theater in New Spain, the *Coliseo* in Puebla. The first program in this "Comedy Circus" was called *My Lady Above All.*

It was Easter of 1761 and society, though dazzled as the curtain opened, missed neither the pearl headdress worn by Señora Almendaro nor Señorita Rivadeneyra's new dress. Lace veils and stolen glances would cause comment for many Sundays, in many salons.

Luxury was to be found in every detail. Puebla families took pride in being rich and showed it in their façades, porches, carriages, furniture and dinnerware.

Puebla overcame the economic problems caused by the prohibition of trade between the colonies and the growing imports from the metropolis. They created new production techniques and converted workshops into modern industries. Their inventiveness transformed their work methods; they installed the first lightning rods, a first machine activated by water and various printing presses. Cotton and wool cloth production allowed for growth even during unstable times.

Built as an 18th-century inn, the Hostal de Velasco salon was sumptuously redecorated in the 19th century. Damask-covered walls, gilded Louis 15th and Louis 16th-style furnishings and French mirrors reveal the magnificence of the period.

Puebla was being banished from the main commercial routes, but the fortunes consolidated in the previous century didn't suffer a dent. The splendor of the façades and interiors, the opulence and adornment spoke for themselves. In 1760, the silver guild erected an obelisk in the *Zócalo*, to commemorate the ascension of Charles III to the throne.

Golden reflections of the 18th century's most prosperous era in the Hostal de Velasco. Furnishings are in the Louis 15th-style.

It is during the 18th century that a unique Puebla style, not to be found anywhere else, emerged. Everybody —either to conform or to compete— sought to live in a mansion with its very own distinctive personality, like the *Casa de Alfeñique* or the *Casa de los Muñecos*.

Left: Two-storey 18th-century patio in the Hostal de Velasco. Austere, slender black quarry stone columns frame the cut stone fountain lined in talavera tile.

Boundless imagination produced a delirious contrast of materials. The elegant and happy result is the façade of this house at the corner of 2 Oriente and 4 Norte.

171

The most representative mansions of the architectural splendor of the period are the *Casa de Alfeñique* and the *Casa de los Muñecos*. The first was built in 1790 by Architect Santa María Incháurregui for Don Ignacio Morales, grandfather of the painter, Francisco Morales. The house is named for its decorated cornices which are reminiscent of a white sweet called *alfeñique*, made of nougat and egg white, icing sugar and almonds.

The Casa de Alfeñique proudly displays the baroque plaster work that inspired its name. The eaves define the curves; the main balcony swells out three times on its path around the corner.

Right: Detail of the corner of the Casa de Alfeñique with its highly ornamented little tower.

174

The wrought-iron balconies rival the filigreed plaster work of the piers and the brick walls speckled with *talavera*. The *Alfeñique* is a three-storey example of the Churrigueresque-style. Beyond the threshold, three arches are sustained by little pillars set on pedestals depicting various figures. The other galleries are supported on brackets decorated with iron stays. The wealth of pilasters and door frames matches the rich diversity of the exterior. The kitchen and the domestic chapel are famous. An octagonal fountain in the center of the patio completes the opulent ambiance.

Two different shells crown the salon's French doors and the dining room's Chinese lacquered door.

Right: The Andalusian entrance to the Casa de Alfeñique has Mudéjar arches and a cut-stone fountain.

Casa de los Muñecos. Nobles support the multilinear cornice. Stories recount that the de Ovando family caused discord in City Hall when their house rose to be taller than the Casas Reales.
The grotesque figures on the façade walls were said to be teasing the town councilors. Others claim that the talavera figures represent the twelve labors of Hercules.

The *Casa de los Muñecos* is unusual and grandiose. It is named for the sixteen tile mosaics on its façade, depicting gigantic figures mounted on pedestals, which Dr. Palm identifies as the labors of Hercules. Built for Agustín de Ovando y Villavicencio, it was said at the time of its construction that the figures mocked City Hall's prohibition to erect such tall houses.

The grandiose effect is due to its grand scale. The façade consists of three levels: the ground floor, with quarry stone door frames, an intermediate floor, and the main floor with plaster frames. Above the entrance is the framed de Ovando family crest, set off by scrolls and fruit motifs. The mosaic figures complete the facing in which clay alternates with the blue and white, yellow and green mosaics.

From Neoclassic to Art Deco

The 19th and 20th Centuries

G reen, white and red. A triumphal arch of foliage and flowers greets the first leader of the Trigarante Army. Puebla de los Angeles proudly celebrates Mexico's Independence. At last, after the *Te Deum*, the Spanish forces have capitulated: it's a double celebration. *Chiles en nogada* are prepared for Don Agustín de Iturbide.

The 19th century was an interminable succession of struggles and instability. The city that had been the cradle of both the most radical liberals and conservatives would recuperate from one war only to tumble into another one. A nation was inventing itself. During several decades, hordes of uniformed men passed through Puebla, fighting for the Monarchy, Independence, the Republic, Sovereignty... Notices would arrive from the port of Veracruz ordering soldiers to sign up beneath this or that flag. Factories and trade stagnated as everyone adjusted to the conditions and tried to survive, waiting for better times.

There are many accounts of travelers passing through Puebla at this time. The Marchioness Calderón de la Barca tells of the "orderly and clean streets between the great houses and the magnificent churches." Von Humbolt describes the size of the valley and the wealth of its resources.

Detail of the neoclassical portal in the house on the corner of 4 Oriente and 2 Norte shows a sculpted bust of Apollo.

The great diversity of stair styles in 19th-century patios.

posts with mist spires, grillwork curling into spirals, chiseled wood doors crowned with laurel leaves and door knockers shaped like fishes or lions.

Two Puebla architects of the period —Carlos Bello and Eduardo Tamariz— built the hospital and the jail. In the *Palacio del Congreso*, Tamariz used the fin de siècle oriental style. The result is a Puebla type of Mudéjar-style, which was later adopted in other interiors.

A variety of styles were combined as Puebla strove to become a cosmopolitan and contemporary city. This eclectic period borrowed from everywhere, resulting in a wild mix, as rococo might share a house with neo-Gothic or Art Nouveau.

The French influence created a whole lifestyle, which affected decor, clothing, pastry and even language. Privileged sons studied in Europe and brought back new political ideas, and production techniques. Their sisters learned French, played the piano or the mandolin at gatherings while an uncle might recite

The once-famous department store, Las Fabricas de Francia (The French Factories) had a steel frame structure imported from France by the Maurer engineers. Today, it houses the Mary Street Jenkins Foundation, which is dedicated to the conservation of Puebla's cultural heritage.

verse and the *belcanto* master might lead the quartet. Spanish and French wines were imported in barrels and bottled for the family table.

For the Pérez de Salazar family, the day started with bell chimes announcing the seven o'clock mass at the cathedral. They would then walk back to the *Casa del Deán* for a breakfast of sweet rolls, *tamales* and chocolate before leaving for the *hacienda*.

The Solana family would go to the *Concepción,* which was closer. Everyone recognized their horses, adorned with bells. In the evenings, after the Rosary, they would visit relatives and friends. Over a steaming cup and home-made sweets, they would discuss the news of Puebla, Mexico and Spain.

On public occasions, Puebla gentry would put on a frock-coat and plumed hat and go for a drive in a landau or a coupé. They vied for elegance in their homes, their factories and their *haciendas.* Clothing and accessories, such as boots, gloves and hats, were imported from Paris.

Art Nouveau balcony railings harmonize with the neoclassical-style of this house. 19th century.

Next pages: Don Marcelino García Presno's home. The stairs dramatize the magnificent neoclassical patio covered with skylights. The corridor railings surrounding the patio accomodate hanging pots.

Left: An imperial stairway in the neoclassical-style in the Casa de la Reina (the Queen's House) where the Empress Carlota stayed during her visit to Puebla. Framed by two cast-iron lamps, the staircase begins its ascent below a basket handle archway, bordered with a richly decorated frieze of painted and gilded plaster.

The romantic paneling of the ceiling is reflected in the parquet design.

The dining room doors at the back of the corridor —of beveled and engraved glass— allow a view of the walls beyond. Romantic frescos flank the central door.

In the home of the Caso family
—remodeled by Architects Tamariz
and Arpa— the corridor is protected
by a glass roof, forming a shell above
a central niche.

198

199

Spanish Architect Arpa made the Mudéjar-style game room fashionable. This game room has Arab-style embossed plaster and a skirting of tiles imported from the Middle East. The floor and slender columns are made of Tecali onyx.

202

Left: The main salon of the Caso home has French-style paneling on the ceiling and walls; the plaster walls are adorned with romantic motifs. The blue bedroom is upholstered in silk brocade. The furniture is quilted in the fashion of the period. The combination of furniture styles illustrates the Puebla penchant for eclectic collecting.

A Victorian carved wood partition. Traditionally, the family business office was located on the ground floor of the Puebla home.

Casa Cué. The Art Deco bathroom skylight has a two-tailed mermaid with a Botticelli face.

Right: Dining room furniture is Art Nouveau, with a striking table centerpiece and lamp. Romantic frescos adorn the walls.

A mixture of styles: from romantic to Art Nouveau. Meissen and Sèvres pieces and bibelots below a ceiling painting of a nymph.

The corridor in Don José Cué's house was remodeled by Architect Carlos Bello in 1905. The lead-plated wrought railing is topped with talavera flower pots; the wood partition leads to the dining room, which combines romantic with Art Deco.

206

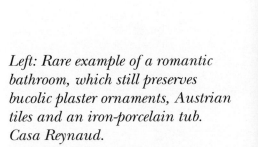

Left: Rare example of a romantic bathroom, which still preserves bucolic plaster ornaments, Austrian tiles and an iron-porcelain tub. Casa Reynaud.

The romantic bedroom, perhaps belonging to the teenager of the family, is furnished with a rosewood bed. The linen sheets are embroidered with Bruges lace. The walls are framed in rocaille.

The music salon in the Casa Reynaud has a view on the Reforma. Decorated in pastel tones, it has heavy damask and velvet curtains trimmed and edged with cords and tassels. Plaster frames and musical scenes seek to balance decorative elements.

Parakeets in the corridor of the Rangel home.

Right: Salon inspired by Versailles in Veronese green, with stucco adornments and paneling. Belgian mirrors reflect the Baccarat chandelier. The mahogany doors, carved by Puebla artisans, are hung with silk curtains, edged with cording and tassels. In the center of the room is a gold-plated bronze clock, a gift from Emperor Maximilian and Empress Carlota.

Angelopolitana
Ciuitas